Dirt Sandwich

Dirt Sandwich

POEMS

LINDA ANNAS FERGUSON

Press 53
Winston-Salem, NC

Press 53
PO Box 30314
Winston-Salem, NC 27130

First Edition

A TOM LOMBARDO POETRY SELECTION

Copyright © 2009 by Linda Annas Ferguson

Cover design by Kevin Watson

Cover photograph, "Dirt," copyright © 2009 by Bee Brady

Author photo by Cynthia Yacapraro

Printed on acid-free paper

ISBN 978-0-9824416-6-4

Acknowledgments

Grateful acknowledgment is made to the editors of the following publications in which these poems first appeared, some in slightly different versions:

The Southern Poetry Anthology: Volume 1: South Carolina
(Texas Review Press)
    "The First Night"

Twenty: South Carolina Poetry Fellows (Hub City Writers Project)
    "Adopted, Age Five"

Eating Her Wedding Dress (Ragged Sky Press)
    "Sundown"

Award Winning Poems (North Carolina Poetry Society)
    "The River"

Wild Goose Poetry Review: Volume 3, Issue 2
    "I Wanted to Hear Her Howl"
    "Journey"

Solo Café: Teachers and Students (Solo Press)
    "Tower of Babel"

Poetry Society of South Carolina Yearbook
    "Woman Suffers a Miscarriage After Learning of Her
    Sister's Death"

Gibbes Museum of Art: Poets and Painters
    "Leaving"

Poetry Society of Georgia: Volume LXXIV
    "The First Night"

South Carolina Poetry Initiative Chapbook Web Anthology
(University of South Carolina)
    "Nine Days at Sea"
    "Dance of Solitude "

Southern Mist (Old Mountain Press)
    "Catching Fireflies"

Some of these poems have been previously published in the
following chapbooks:

Last Chance to Be Lost
Kentucky Writers Coalition, 2004

Stepping on Cracks in the Sidewalk
Finishing Line Press, 2006

for Shirley and Betty

and in loving memory of
Neil Ferguson (1942-2009)

Contents

I

II

III

I

The First Word

In the beginning, the world was ownerless,
everything wanting a name. Adam,
the first miracle, awoke from sleep
unable to explain how it felt to be struck dumb

by beauty, lips quivering with unearned privilege
and questions, words forming in his brain,
the first sound more of a whimper,
a living thing, aching and untamed.

How did he know what to utter, which
imperfect vowel belonged to each
orchid or orangutan, emerging monikers
born from moans, murmurs and subtle sighs.

He strained to fill his tongue with every thought,
unable to identify the pleasure, raw
with newness and power, mouth parting—
their genesis and tone feeling true.

Breech Birth

I had a hard time getting the beginning right,
brought with me no memories, no measure
for what is true, only this knowledge
of being far away, scissors separating me

from important dreams—cutting the leash
of sleep, like a root slashed from a wound
that took a long time to heal, scar still there.

I was created in one heartbeat given away
in conceiving, lovers aware only of the throb
of night, sweet sweat falling on raised flesh
like dew forming itself.

My style was feet first and hurried
like an appointment I must keep,
pushing, pushing toward aloneness,
then drowning in boundless space.

I came into this world with nothing
but a name, a gentle voice to greet me,
scrubbed hands delivering my life
from perfect patterns and symmetry,

bright crosses of light nailed to the ceiling,
hurting my eyes, an abrupt breath rushing
into me, the pure weight of it filling
my body with a sudden urge to cry.

Genesis

For eight straight days
Adam summoned all the animals,
each name calling itself
as if it already existed—
squirrel, skunk, camel;

falling asleep now and then
until his own voice woke him—
muskrat, mink, mandrill.

Words lived in his bones
touched his tongue, still wild,
a slow burning freedom
inside every sound.

How he longed for more words
to love, thought they could save
him from the wet falling sky,
from red flaming sunsets,
from all that hadn't come yet.

Staying Alive

Outside, birds neaten their nests
and just by being, bring something
into the world: bird, nest, egg, song.

On this side of the window
I have just made my bed, fluffed
the pillow behind my back
to compose a score for human voices.

I wish that words could change
our external world, physics telling us
we are in flux, everything an illusion,

skin replacing itself once a month,
the whole skeleton in only three,
the heaviness of our bodies, water,
keeping us from floating away.

When does the body decide
not to do the work anymore, no longer
feel the lightness of song, play of poetry,
soar of sex, satisfying our thoughts?

I test the new sounds that speak
of endings, yet born on the breath,
each syllable an innocence
heeding time's yesses and nos,

my human form made anew
every second, yet leaving as I exhale.
Words disappearing into thin air.

The First Night

He took one of his ribs and closed up the flesh at that place.
Genesis 2:21

As we lie
side by side,
strangers,

my fingers search
your back,
feel the jagged edge

of the rib you gave
in your sleep
to make me.

For this night
I want
to put it back,

until I am
bone of your bone
and flesh

of your flesh
and you feel whole again.
In the morning

I will open the wound
so gently
you may not hear me

rise
and tiptoe
out of the garden.

7

The First Morning

The sun stands on the wall,
follows it down to my window,
waits on the sill next to the bed
until your hard sleep softens.

The night has been long.
Cold rolls down the valley,
wind carving white curves.
The snow stiffens.

You came to my door hungry
from solitude, said the world
left you, asked me for crumbs
of my hours. It is morning,

the first day. Your eyes arc with light,
climb the surprised sky, then slow,
remembering me on your new earth.
I don't want to know if I am

not all you expected. This cool sheet
is my pleasure, your hair warm
against the sun. This is enough
to satisfy the body's chill.

Beginnings

*...she took of the fruit thereof, and did eat, and gave
also unto her husband with her; and he did eat.*

Genesis 3:6

Now that he is strong enough
to be weak, he climbs
the tree he fears
where promises wait.

There is more love
than they can waste,
thoughts become music,
a song with no name.

He writes the last line first,
the next and the next
until he is her beginning
and they learn each other's sound.

He asks her to stay
close beside him—
so soft are the reasons
he folds into her palm.

She pins them to leaves,
temporary stars,
and prays for those unborn
who have no sky that burns.

Something About Morning

Morning, modesty
in the cool air,
a wet mist warming
on the window.

Panes divide the sun,
measure every shadow.
I have slept naked,
the flesh exposed.

My dream shatters
when the rays pierce
glass. The rest
of my life stretches—

beyond my body.
Later, I will
spend time
trying to gather light.

Innocence

...and they realized they were naked.

Genesis 3:7

When I was three, I could write
my name, scrawled it on doors,
walls, furniture, floors.

When Mama took my crayons,
I fingered it in the cold sweat
of windowpanes, paused to dot
the "i," an eyehole to the moon.

I can still hear the wane
of her warnings against making
a mottled mess, the letters

quick shapes of order,
impermanent in water, a wash
of feathery light, taking it all away.

I remember innocence,
its quiet withdrawal.
Shame showed it to me,

made it feel like pain,
Mother, teaching me, as I
squatted in the bathtub,
the embarrassment of bodies.

I remember the clumsiness
of my first kiss, as Daddy rapped
his knuckles on the kitchen casement—

to break our embrace. There are
no absolutes in the dark recesses
of virginity, the flooding tunnels

of the body. It is not a gift
we can give back to each other.
I can hear my mother's "Don't—

touch," as I poked
at splintering fissures of frost
on the other side of the window—

and all that enchanted me
about the broken. The weight
of awe in the tip of my finger
could crack glass.

Topless Dancer

She embraces her own body,
cups a glitter-laden breast,
a golden moon. Dance
is the way she speaks,
embodies what she can't say.

Flesh chilled by the room—
the spotlight coaxes her to the stage
like a sun-warmed place. She teases
a silver pole, her only partner,
holds on as if it were human.

Men at the bar grin each time she licks
her lips, or the blue, bleeding heart
tattooed beneath her rhinestone thong
is exposed with subtle motions; trapped
stories in her hands trying to create
a choreographed happy ending.

She almost believes the smiles
she receives, as if the soft edges
of her stare could conjure all she needs.
The truck driver in the front row
caresses the curve of his beer bottle,
wipes its cold sweat through his hair.

It's like a feather boa, this weight
of nakedness. She takes it with her
as she bows to whistles and applause.
In the shower, she washes until the water
is cold and her bones feel clean, scrubs
away all the eyes that have touched her.

Dance of Solitude

...but from the tree of the knowledge of good and evil you shall not eat,
for in the day that you eat from it you will surely die.

Genesis 2:17

Dying begins with instinct,
a reflex in the womb,
slight flinch of foot,
a discontented elbow.

Born kicking air
before we can breathe,
we want all the years
we can get of dying,

not knowing how
much time we have
to practice, no
specifics on endings.

The first step we learn
is leaving, trading Edens
for uncertainties, even leaving
love when dancing feels like dying.

We all choreograph our separations,
two divided by two makes one—
learn to keep the rhythm, stay in step
even though there is no music.

This is the dance of solitude.
We'll show you our feet
with the sores on the soles, legs
kicking high as they will reach.

The Origin of Entropy

Eden has gotten accustomed
to the absence of laughter.
Early risers have left footprints
in pliable sand, shadows,
spaces without embodiment,
follow them from place to place.

A sudden wind uncurls at the feet
of olive trees, erases where they've been.
Rotting almond shells empty
their short lives. The desert tells
its shore stories, a carnage red sunset

submerged in undisturbed earth, dawn
bleeding its dense dew. Everything
is drenched with endings, alive with dying
in a world that takes itself apart, forces,
certain of their chore, accountable
only to their measurable god.

Everything Real Is an Illusion

Cold passes through the ark's walls
as Noah lies awake in early morning,
imagines he can enter objects by choice;
chair, floor, window, like a sudden chill.

Dawn hovers dense and opaque
beyond the sill. The cool gray of a dove
with one half-turn—slices through it,
a color so dull he can't decide
where separation begins.

Dew dries on an olive leaf left on his bed
of hay as it yields to gentle change. His mind
succumbs to half-sleep, inside this world,
then another, where thoughts are weightless
and dreams warm the walls of his body.

It is here he learns to trust the translucent, lucid,
flies without wings, floats over reflections
of clearing sky, walks with uncertain sea legs
across field after field of glassy water,
their glittering lights solid as land.

Barefoot

… so Noah knew that the waters were abated from off the earth.
Genesis 8:11

We couldn't wait
for the first of May, the day
we would shed our shoes,
discover earth with bare feet.
We loved dirt, digging holes
in gray clay, often straying
beyond watchful eyes to creeks
and culverts, catching crawfish.

We kicked dandelions along the way,
blew their seed to the wind,
each one a tiny parachute,
fragile life floating to the ground
without sound. I asked impartial petals
of odorless daisies about the future,
picking a perfect world apart…
he loves me, he loves me not, never

venturing past my worriless youth,
so far away from the thought
of mortal remains, unaware of decay
and the smell of time. Without remorse,
we poured salt on snails to watch
them melt, yet never thought
about death, armed with innocence
and an endless then, but I remember when

I first felt sorrow. My brother was tying
Mama's sewing thread to June bug legs,
flying them like a living kite. When the sun
was gone, and their iridescence shone
no longer, one severed leg lay to the side
still tied to the string. I took it home
in a fist of clover, where dreams
of wingless things wounded my sleep.

Rainbows Are Real

I have set my bow in the clouds, and it shall be a sign
of the covenant between me and the earth....

Genesis 9.13

If you walk toward one, it will move away,
existence relative to the rain, the angle
of light traveling, slowing as it goes
through water, scattering into color,
then bending back to our eyes.

Once I saw a rainbow while flying,
looking down from the sky, not an arc,
but a complete circle, the plane's silhouette
in the center. Pilots call it a "glory."

I wonder if this was the way one first appeared
to God, His magnified shadow hovering
over muddy land and multitudes of dead bodies
like the last dark cloud as it drained itself,

a halo, whole and unbroken, cast when the sun
was low, a symbol for the end of devastation
and downpours of paternal lessons, yet
bewildering enough to be a bringer of blessings.

Endings

...and the waters shall never again become a flood to destroy all flesh.

Genesis 9:15

You cannot get caught
in the same rain twice.

A transparent pearl
will not cling to your lash
when you close your eyes
to drink from the sky.

The heavens will not descend
like music. Wet notes
will not shatter when they touch
the strain of your tongue.

You will not notice how rain
tastes so strangely of nothing.
Your thirst will not be quenched
if you console every cloud.

People will pass all around
but they will see only
how the sun breaks on your back
as you walk away.

Tower of Babel

What do you think was the last word
spoken before language was confused,
what final opinion offered unopposed
in the original tongue of Adam?

Were they all still standing around
that day in the rubble of stone
after speech was confounded,
not knowing what to do next,

the only humans available to fire
the first bricks after the flood,
the foundation unfinished
before they built higher floors?

Did they draw designs in the clay,
make their handprints like children
creating something permanent,
just before the tower collapsed

over the land, wander away, babbling,
bewildered why no one could understand
each other, and in spite of everything,
trust their own incoherent voices?

Losing Touch

*...and from there the Lord scattered them abroad
over the face of the whole earth.*

Genesis 11:9

My only cousin lives in a condo
on the California coast,
its name, Kona Kai,
claiming "shelter from the wind."

In unexplained photos she sends,
there's no evidence of the ocean.
Façades and dark windows separate us
from the calm or rage of the tide.

She hasn't called in years. She's
angry at remarks no one remembers.
We're the only two left, except
some aunts and a crazy uncle.

An old car that could hold a family
of four is parked in front of an open door,
the road divided by lanes going both ways
like a life with two endings.

There's not a cloud, no threat
of rain in the idyllic sky, not a clue
to imply why she hides
behind this wall of falling light.

In a picture-perfect world, we would walk
on the beach, seashells in hand, talk,
write each other's name in the sand
on the shore always protected from the wind,
pose for each other, flippant,
as if flirting with a camera, a breeze
brushing away a lock of hair
that used to worry her brow.

II

On Awakening

My days are disappearing like smoke.
My body burns like glowing coals.

Psalms 102:3

Needles of light prick my sleep
as I rise beside a cold campfire,
stir black coals with a hickory stick,
blow into ashes. They whirl
in wispy gray, float so weightless
they pass straight through
open palm and closed fingers.

I whisper to disappearing fragments
as if they could remember
the stories of our lives we shared
circling warmth in the dark,
dreams we forgot on waking.
"Will I miss my life?" I ask
as they descend, silence filling

earth's holes and hollows, shallow
graves waiting for charred remains
of limbs, leaves, a tree that once lived,
as they dance with dust motes
in dew-filled slanted rays
just inches away from fresh kindling,
the memory of heat, of sizzling cinders.

Advice To My Younger Self

Do not offer yourself casually
to the woman you want to be.
Once you follow her,
there's no going back.

She will call to you
from her place of never enough,
ask you to write poetry
to sunsets, another dying day.

You will erase words that don't work,
ink disappearing as mysterious
as memory—that miracle
of mind to remember itself.

Ask her first if she can love
primal and complete.
She's no safer than you
from the end of her life.

First Memory of Mama's Knees

Her children arise and call her blessed...
Proverbs 31:28

I fit into their back when I was three,
hid behind her skirt, chewed on its hem
when strangers came. She held me
on her lap, head pulled to the pillow
of her breast with the hush of her hand.

She kept everything inside, breathing out
only sighs. Once, she let herself laugh.
It started like a struggle, until
her whole body shook in a stifled gasp.

It has been eleven years since she left.
I live 300 miles from her grave, dig
through old photos, dying to write
a decent poem, something lasting—
while others read only her carved name.

Mornings, I open my eyes, wake
from dreams of funeral roses, dozens
of flowers she never once received in life,
petals falling like prayers come apart.

How composed she fell into death,
her silence thriving, a living thing, a legacy
to hide behind, a hem to hang onto
on this journey out of myself.

Best Losses of Our Lives

The world is daily robbed of stories.
We wait in long lines at funeral homes
looking for them, doting over death,
the ultimate unsolved mystery,

boring each other with our histories,
sharing abandoned beginnings,
the best losses of our lives,
each retelling so real and original.

What perfect sense we make, shaking
the hands of the grieving, comfort and support
cut short by the black-sheep cousin behind us,
the only one without regret or remorse,

butting in as we compose our condolences,
words weighed for their brief worth,
wanting them to be warm and consoling
as if dying is what happens to others.

Jammin' With Janis Joplin

...eat, and to drink, and to be merry...
Ecclesiastes 8:15

The first thing you think of is sex
when you hear her scorch the air
with *"Honey, get it while you can."*
But we all know "It" was more than that.

She was only twenty-seven when she checked out
at the Landmark Motel, the fourth of October,
1970, closed her eyes, snapped the heels
of her blue leather boots as if she were Dorothy
nearing the narrow yellow brick road.

She didn't stick around to see if the Lord
would buy her a less meaningful *Mercedes-Benz*,
the last song she sang, will waning,
the Emerald City, a place still undefined.

Some say she didn't die, but was buried alive
in music—while others spread her ashes
over the Pacific, tiny pieces, decibels
above the gentle arpeggios of the water—
wanting her, the ocean never deep enough.

Woman Suffers a Miscarriage
After Learning of Her Sister's Death

Did she read her paper alone
over tea, begin to complain
at the overpriced cost of plain
white bread, not hearing the phone
because a robin had flown
into the kitchen windowpane?
Did she notice the bloodstain
on the glass, the feather on

the sill, the sound of the blow,
labor over a crossword,
leave blank what she didn't know,
hum an old tune she had heard,
or think of the embryo
small in her womb like a bird?

Questions I Never Asked My Mother

I applied my heart to know…
Ecclesiastes 7:25

Sometimes I talk to your hat
when I need to know something
I never asked when you were here.
What would you have done
differently with your only life
if you could have done anything at all?

Would you have had regrets
never to know the dreams
of your unborn children?
We all nursed your milk,
each one of us a beginning.

You showed me a photo when you
were my age, posed in a stylish cloche
cocked to one side, the only time
I ever saw you in a hat. It was
handed down from your mother
who was married three times

and wore a different fedora
every Sunday. I think I said,
"How pretty you were once,"
but I might have
just mouthed the words.

Sundown

I have decided.
I will leave barefoot,
not even a suitcase,
shoes under your table.

We sit straight, poised,
our shadows stretch stiff
across the floor.
I drink a last cup of light

and remember how we
watched the coming night,
forced days to come and go.

But now, when the dark
presses flat against our window,
we lie naked on the bed,

our clothes in the closet,
bodiless.

Goodbyes

I stand on the threshold
in a farewell embrace,
wanting only
to take your pain.

You want me to have
the photo album.
I fit all our history
in the back seat of the Buick.

I don't tell you I'm tired of taking
pictures, always on the other side
of the lens, expected to record
the years, never on any page.

You hand me a daisy. I frame
a final image from the window
of the closing car door,
remember our first date.

You gave me royal asters
and angel's breath in my doorway,
as if to have anything
you had to give all away.

The River

Go down to the river,
put in a thin hand,
drink the reflection of stars.

As you gather the gold,
notice how it empties itself
of light, hold in your palm
all you never tasted.

Let your lips remember
the past, swallow
the dark and the cold.

Tell the river
how you loved me.

When you take back your hand
watch the ripple leave its center
and disappear.

Leaving

I feel myself disappearing
into all that lies ahead,
the hood of the car
parting morning air.

The rain and I
have long conversations
about what makes the future
rich, the past cheap.

Melodies of Van Morrison
drizzle over me.
My ordinary heart
beats out its sameness.

I long for more than
forgetting myself in songs.
Somewhere miles away,
the sun is setting.

The highway believes
in endings. Its broken lines
point deep into the distance,
like painted white bones

laid end to end, drone
their dreary goodbye,
goodbye,
goodbye.

What We Leave Behind

... much study is a weariness of the flesh.
Ecclesiastes 12:12

It's humbling to be human,
to have an examined life
turned over so many times
it feels leathery.

I walk the beach remembering
the smooth bohemian I meant to be.
An old man calls to me
from the concrete slab of a condo.

He's offering me something,
plums rotting in a bowl, juice
seeping from their wrinkled skin.

Waves scratch their scars
into the shore. Varicose purple
streaks the sky. I leave a shell

for a young woman asleep
in a hammock, an oyster
still silky and iridescent
by her open hand.

Imperfection

It's all the broken things washed up
on the shore that I adore, driftwood
tumbled into art by salt and sea,
fractured shells, dirty and stained, rust
running down the legs of the pier.

It's easy to find imperfections,
gritty muck stuck to the seat of my jeans,
names scribbled with a finger
in the packed sand, Larry loves …
the second name washed away in the tide,

…footprints leading away, side by side.

Photograph in the Garden

My beloved is to me a cluster of henna blossoms...
Song of Solomon 1:14

At first she is nervous, hands
folded across her lap, knees
pressed together as if life
is intended only for others, then
her fingertip begins to fondle light,
a pointed toe stirs the sand,
curved arch of a foot relaxes,
her hand waving away the heat.
Butterflies hover—

over poised petals, ready to open.
Roses remind her of innocence,
their layers of unexposed lips
oblivious to whose thoughts they're in.
There is power in the silence
just before the click of the camera
that captured her eyes
closing like falling blossoms.

After Warmth

Song of Solomon 2: 10-11

A star   falling   breaks our sentences,
conversation wanes about the weather,
words more content unspoken,

as we watch from our window
across a winter-stained field, the demise
of anything making our chests rise.

Frost   spreads its   impermanent roots
on the glass. A feather lies frozen
to a leaf on the sill. Thin wings
of fire flutter, trapped in the woodstove.

In spring, the creek will be fat,
bellying its warm way through ice,
around bends and hollows,
breaking   on   rocks.

I make a wish on our stream of fading light
descending to its grave of gravity.
Stars, not yet gone amiss,
stare at me, grant their burning consent.

Dandelions for Virgie, 1930

(for Mother: 1916-1996)

...I must seek him whom my soul loves.
I sought him but did not find him.

Song of Solomon 3:2

Loose threads cling to her clothes
like Beggar's Lice. She clutches
a paper bag, makes her way outside
the cotton mill to eat her lunch alone
on the hill next to the river.

Squirrels at play do not notice her
collecting thistles in a Mason jar,
making flutes from the thinnest reeds,
looking for four-leaf clovers.

Here, she can be anything she wants,
not a linthead, not a weaver,
taken out of school to work,
father dead since she was three.

There's destiny in all the daisies.
"He loves me, he loves me not."
Fate-filled dandelions wait
for whispered words, one quick breath.

At the blow of the whistle,
she carries them intact,
climbs the steps back to the weave room,
a fistful close to her body, wishes
still forming in her fourteen-year-old breast.

Catching Fireflies

"How do they know I'm coming?"
my daughter asks into the mouth
of an empty Mason jar,

her fourteen-year-old mind wrapping
itself like closing fingers around
the idea of an easy answer.

I watch a captive firefly flutter
against the clear acrylic lid
of my Q-tip box

remember when I was her age,
half-child, half-woman,
too busy chasing things
to listen to instinct.

Hands parting a curtain of dew—
she takes the mystery from me
like an acceptable answer,
a pulsating light in a tiny prison,
holds it up to the almost dark.

Temporary pleasures are never enough.
She wants all the fire she can hold
grabbing at the night with both fists,

unaware of her own impending destiny
preparing to pounce, a reaching hand
ready to catch her by surprise,

the sudden grasp of something larger,
closing deliberately around her,
time staring through transparent walls.

The Steel Bridge

My bride, you have stolen my heart with one glance of your eyes…
Song of Solomon, 4:9

"1936, steel bridge, wedding day,"
are the only words on the back of the photo
I hold in my hand. Mama gone
eleven years now, the picture still alive
with the story she told so many times.

I am the child not even conceived of yet,
but can see by her eyes how shy she was,
Dad's hand, slung too familiar over her shoulder,
hanging near one breast like a man on the make.

Moments before they stopped to pose—
her story goes (I can still hear her telling it),
he handed her a stick of gum. She let it slip
between a crack in the creosoted slats,

swayed to watch it fall hundreds of feet below.
His arm, outstretched, offered to steady her.
Later, they will take the trail to the ravine,
hop from rock to rock, her shoe will get lodged
in a crevice, then carried downstream by the current,

waters now flowing some seventy years away
from this snap of a shutter, from the permanence
of steel and stone, the empty space that spans
the breadth between my world and theirs.

Strange how a river can shift, change its shape,
curve and turn, alter its course in order
not to be tamed or claimed by anyone,
though it marries stream and creek at every fork.

Promises

I.

The two brown paper bags Mama left with
contained all she thought
she'd ever need, her twenty year-old
fiancé's arm around the shoulder
of a second-hand coat nobody missed.

As they drove away, the girl
she once knew grew smaller
in the rear view mirror as she said "I do"
to the road ahead. Her mother, needing her
weekly pay, wanted her to stay
another year, waved a weak goodbye.

II.

She called her husband "Fat"
like his friends in the mill, added it
to a vocabulary of new words:
spouse, sex, vow ...
to whisper to the future.

Over time, five children were born,
three others died. Motherhood was a religion
she learned to be faithful to, smoothing bread
each morning, a solemn ceremony before dawn,
humming hymns to the formless dough.

Her unlotioned hands dabbed liniment
on a child's soft bruises, simple solutions
for others' wounds, beating her own pain
into sweet cake batter, every grin
above an icing-coated chin consoling her again.

III.

She wrote on blank pages
in the back of her Bible, listed
what she deemed the best moments
of her children's lives, one winning
a bicycle, age twelve, another
finding a sapphire ring by the road.

They all searched for pieces of her
after her death, opened shoeboxes
buried in the bottom of her wardrobe,
found the remains of babies' teeth,
life-filled locks of blonde hair,
their own birth certificates
held together with a safety pin.

III

Awakening To Myself

Scenes from dreams play in my head,
each character a likeness of me. In one,
I have lost my purse, my identity, drift
from place to place. In another, my son,
my sister, my lover, are wanderers too.

Some say, in the mirror of the mind,
they are also me. I write details
in my diary, just in case dreams are true.
I dreamed I wore a wig, the perfect hair
to match the myriad of masks I create
for the mirror, yet I imagine I make them
for others, as I dab mascara, accent my eyes.

When I turn two mirrors at angles,
multiple reflections glare back, my array
of faces one within another, within another,
within another. Countless hands reach out—
all at the same moment, We touch,
fingertip to fingertip, leave prints on the glass.

Confirmation

... seek, and ye shall find...

Matthew 7:7

Hours go by in the sky.
She sits in a cathedral of trees.
The elders have sent the student
to learn alone, to no longer
look with just her eyes.

She thinks of how
her two-week-old puppies
have finally opened their eyes,
how her grandfather died

with his eyes open, how
some people sit with their eyes
wide in the darkness at bedtime
waiting for sleep to come.

How close the words sleep
and seek. If she wanted to,
she could close her eyes
and stay awake a whole night.

How To Forgive

Take a sip of wine,
let it worry your mouth.
Open up the dirty window.
When moonlight is weeping
on the lawn, scatter crackers
and bread crumbs, scream,
throw stones at the stars.

Imagine another love.

Throws stones at the stars,
and bread crumbs. Scream
on the lawn, scatter crackers.
When moonlight is weeping,
open up the dirty window.
Let it worry your mouth,
take a sip of wine.

Midsummer's Eve: The Bonfire

We sit in a circle. Faces stare into each other.

Fire illumines how the years singe our features, we feed it
our shared hours, time burned in effigy, a fitting ritual
for the longest day with its extra minutes to spare.

The house and barn are mysterious in shadow,
a colt's eyes eerie in the dark corral.
We all hold hands, prance like show horses, weave

through the woods and out again with sporadic displays
of nickers and neighs, growing older, dancing, becoming
young, like the waxing and waning of the moon.

When heat hovers over glowing coals, we offer up
unwanted hurts that smolder, poems and photos
that kindle regret, all we hope to purge from the past.

The letter I wrote you four years ago, but never mailed,
curls its edges inward. The words that pleaded
to be read, until I loved how I hated them, disappear

into a hot dot of light. At midnight, we float on our backs
in the pool, weightless as ash under the cool gaze
of stars in a wide country sky, forgiveness

a distant heaven that burns. Disintegrated paper
and charred snapshots whisper from seared cinders.
The veils are thin between the worlds.

Prodigal Son

My fear is that you will disappear
into a world that makes strangers,
where shadows swallow what we love,
as if each year were only a thought.

No need to promise me anything.
Promise instead to your life-to-come
what you really want—
to be the one you can rely on.

Disappearance requires no causes.
You will be everywhere else but here,
living a future moment, the one that
could happen, the one that will get away.

Sooner than you can imagine, you
will be my age reading a bedtime story
to your own son, who will speak up
when the emperor wears no clothes.

In due course, I will be a story in time,
invisible to your children, part of a past
in photo albums and portraits,
while they test tree limbs and gravity,

barely holding on to a rope, digging holes
to China. You'll want more for them
than for yourself as they play too close
to fire, despite your worried warnings.

Could I Say

"What's missing?"
when there's no language for it,
no chance to warn my children
who are becoming too much like me

not calling my own mother
for months because she
couldn't make it easy,
couldn't choose my path to follow

or tender life's wordless moments,
borrowed from a love held and lost,
morning light laid on a pillow next to me?
If I die today, the bed will not be made,

bills not paid, thirteen million dollar
lottery ticket left unchecked, spyware
staring from the Internet.
Will someone say to my family

and friends at the funeral—
we all live and leave with regrets,
wish we had loved without neglect
or are there no words for that?

Waiting at the Well

...he would have given you living water...

John 4:10

It is light that makes water
a mirror, the surface a glass canvas
I reveal myself to, awed
by the sky reducing itself for me.

In the reflection, trees
are a cold green. The wet sun
penetrates the water. The deep
gives itself to its long-boned fingers.

The other side of the mirror
holds the memories of all
that has been seen, the way
the earth holds each seed.

I am a measurer
of all that is fleeting, turning
over liquid soil, drinking
out of the fleshed cups of my hands.

Nine Days at Sea

And there were three to bear witness in earth,
the Spirit, and the water, and the blood...

1 John 5:8

"A poet died today,"
the two-week-old newspaper reports
from beneath lifeless bodies of black bass
as I filet them, stew for the crew,

slide the slippery entrails and eyes to one side,
wash away blood, lay them out by the rail
like corpses on a slab, while others flail and lash,
shaking their small bucket of water and salt.

The poet's name was Barbara,
biology maintaining she was mostly water,
connected to all leaving things by the sea,
by rain and rivers, sweat and saliva.

The ocean and sky have glared at me so long
I feel bodiless. The deep, a communal soup,
watches all my motions, the surge and ebb of me.

Gray backs of dolphin surface
and disappear. Light, slight as a minnow,
dives into the dark of the liquid horizon.

Cold Black Water

Pretend there is no blue hen
drowned in the horse's trough
when you wake from your dream
of breaking eggs, no death

to surprise you, no black mirror
to swallow your reflection
when you look long
into the wakeless water

as if something valuable were lost,
the morning sun rising
like a floating heart,
over the abandoned cornfield

while a cock dusts his feathers
in the dirt, pecks grit
to grind in his gizzard, sizes up
a mate to pick from the flock,
crows in another day.

The ghost of a weightless God
haunts the heat of your hand,
as you stare into ordinary air,
stir the lifeless flies.

Dirt Sandwich

Whoever eats my flesh and drinks my blood has eternal life....
John 6:54

My friend Sheila told me she ate
a dirt sandwich the thirteenth year
of her husband Hank's sickness, as he lay
in their living room in his hospital bed.
Outside on her knees, she heaped spoons

of red Carolina clay onto Wonder Bread,
taking solemn communion with the God
she prayed to every day as she changed
Hank's diapers, wiped puréed soup
and baby food from his mouth and chin.

This was after she dragged his atrophied body
to healers, churches in deserted theaters,
but before their trailer was reduced
to dust by a tornado, everything
she ever loved pitted by sand, her panties

draped on the mailbox, curious neighbors
picking through the particulars of her life,
piling them into the back of a pick-up truck,
spatulas, bras, broken bowls, the spoon
she used to make the dirt sandwich.

She could just have easily spit when pity
filled her throat, but waited, breathing
away the dread until the dry sacrament
became mud, submissive on her tongue.
She could tell you about swallowing hard,

before she washed the grit down
with a glass half-full
of warm wine and years before
her kitchen chair, carried by the wind,
hung upside down in the chinaberry tree.

Conversation About Dirt

It is our duty to honor the dirt.
We are born from decay,
the dust of sulfur, cobalt,
copper, silver and gold,
a few drops of dew.

Bones owe their beginnings
to the beds of the earth.
Ribs, fingers, feet, elbows
formed from common compost.

We cannot deny how we came
from darkness,
deep in slumber, dreams
rooted around rocks.

It is our duty to honor the dirt,
gather around the holes we dig,
erect two crossed sticks
to mark where we mattered.

We Will Always Have the Poor

who wait outside the cities' gates,
the blind, the lame, the unlovable,
pleading for meals or healing,
our discomfort not enough to bless
those shamed by pity, concealing
our dis-ease if our eyes should meet
those starving on the street, while we beg

as if for alms on our knees in prayer.
There is such poverty in our words
so drained by doubt. Heads bowed,
we make generous vows, spend ourselves
on worry, as if it's all we're worthy of,
"please," a word we've coined,
holding up our empty palms.

Lost and Found

Five years ago, I lost my purse, yet
I still think about it, how I felt erased
by the person who found it,
didn't turn it in, stole my identity.

I had lost who I was, as if that bag,
which held a license to drive,
replaceable papers, a tarnished
1949 dime, were what I called *me*.

That night, I dreamed I worked
in a department store, responsible
for the lost and found. Greedy people
came by, claimed what wasn't theirs.

The elderly, the lonely, want someone
to call on the phone when they come home
from graveyards where their friends
lie among acres of lost names.

Sometimes I ask myself, *Who am I?*
What can my feeble words say
to the future lost in the pages
of faded books at a yard sale

next to a bag woman looking for old purses,
a virtual license to rummage, pocketing
a 1949 dime? I can feel the smallness
of us all as it falls from her fingers.

Adopted, Age Five

I will not leave you all alone like orphans...
John 14:18

His new mother has left him
waiting on the stoop
to go inside to buy clothes
he doesn't want.

This is a day when everything
is wrong. He thinks of his distant bed,
a pillow with just the right softness,
his real mother who gave him away,

how he fit into the folds of her skirt
when strangers came, chewed
the hem as he had done before
when she didn't mind, thinks

of his older brother, almost fifteen,
coming home from school to find him—
gone, toys left by a door, except for
the plastic soldier now in his hand,

thinks of his mother's eyes, far away
as the day his father died, how they
stared past him as if he wasn't there.
The door of the store swings open,

arms rustling with paper packaging
wrap around him, lift
his pliable bones, hold him close,
this soft, larger body stealing his.

Innocence II

Innocence has no opposite,
no true antonym, nothing
to name what it is not.

Some suggest "guilt" would serve,
or maybe "finding fault," going back
to the Garden of Eden to place blame
on the first ones to know nakedness.

Others say Genesis is a poem
about choice, shame the leaf
we put on, even claim innocence
is something that can be stolen,

the way death robs us of our bodies,
peels them away like clothes, until we
feel as exposed as Eve, empty enough
to beget seven billion souls.

Prostitute Turns Forty

He who is without sin among you,
let him be the first to throw a stone at her.
John 8:7

Her world has aged fast, changes
when she's not looking, skin
loosing its smoothness,
mirror revising matter.

She knows how time can't be seduced
by her will or reduced to a trick
of the mind, forever slowing,
then speeding up when she needs it most.

Each hour is a gauge as a customer
pours wine, gazes at something far away.
Trust turns hard with displeasure
as she moans approval to men
in a world she pretends to master.

Men pretend too, pretend all they need
is an hour, a caress, an embrace,
their lives unlistened to, the boy
inside them still learning limits.

A hard light hurts her eyes as he comes
and goes from the water bowl, washing
away body fluids and significance,
until he leaves by the door on her right
and all that is right is his leaving.

Salvation

The markers on the graves are counting
all of us, the already numb, who scratch
our names in granite. Wounded shadows
watch, drag their hems across the grass.

Bones of mothers survive, rocks piled high
on the dirt in a ring, a necklace of pebbles,
to adorn where wombs give birth to worms
and mold. Time gnaws at the rest of us.

We take them flowers pulled from earth,
grasped in a fist, roots still dangling
from the stems, as if we could replant them,
grow more hours. Their soft petals let go

of their hope for us, fall like closing eyelids
praying for everyone who sleeps and dreams.
We are the ghosts who stand at the foot
of their final beds without speaking.

At dusk, the sun is tired of us measuring
its faithfulness, mingles with the horizon,
paints our sky the color of pinched cheeks
and cheap wine, a silent substitute for paradise.

In the morning, its warmth will come again,
cover our forgiven faces with affection,
dance on diamond-crusted water,
burn its dazzling crosses of light.

Noises in the Living Room

Love is not easily angered... it keeps no record of wrongs....
1 Corinthians 13:7

You were not born yet, my best friend
Sarah said to me *when I was awakened*
one night by noises in the living room.
I was only three.

I had slipped behind a door, watched as
my daddy whipped Mama with a switch
broken from a hickory tree, she whispered

childlike, as we, adults now, pick up sticks,
stems and loose debris from her yard,
beaten to the ground by a battering rain.

Don't you ever talk back to me, her daddy
had stormed as he hit her mama
with the same switch Sarah was sent to pick
that day when she had not obeyed.

But she had known her mother never planned
to use it, stuck it over a doorway in plain sight.
All these years, I've blamed myself for being
the reason it was brought into the house, Sarah said,

each word suffering the pain
of her mother's silence, the mute cry
in her hands as he struck her legs, welts

rising like screams trapped under her skin.
Twigs snap under our feet, the raw scent
of breaking limbs stinging the air we breathe.

69

I Wanted To Hear Her Howl

Mother rarely raised her voice,
only sighed as she picked the eyes
from raw potatoes with fingers
that never knew polish or lotion,

never whined, trapped in the to and fro
of hanging wash on the line, slapping
overalls against the wind, taking them

down again, oblivious to the coarseness
against her skin, never wept as she
cleaned floors, never danced
with a broom, spun around the room.

She scrubbed mud stains with its bristles,
swept dust and crumbs outside into the yard,
browning the green grass beyond the steps
where others said their goodbyes.

Most days and nights, the house held her in,
although the doors were never locked.
She rose early without swearing, stared
out the window where railroad ties began.

Beyond the trance of waving weeds
train whistles declared their leaving,
roaring in her head like a scream.

Receiving Friends

When Mother died, lay in state
in our living room, her love
floated all through the house
the way white carnations
permeate a room with perfume.

She wore a new dress
selected by my sisters, pink
as the flush painted on her face.
One rose rested on her pillow,
growing limp, losing its body.

Well-meaning neighbors filed by
her coffin, crowded the room
with correctness, silent eyes
conveying more than lips could say.

Some hadn't visited us in years.
We shook their hands, oblivious
to whose memories we were in,
sat on the obligatory couch,

wishing Mother could have stayed
just another month, remembering
July, how it welcomed her, warmth
a reminder of how she held us

on her lap until we couldn't be held
anymore, wanting to wield our first fork
or ice cream cone, do everything on our own,
yet hungry for what was already gone.

The Rapture

My son wants to know if a wormhole
is how Elijah was taken into the sky,
as he watches snow whiten the lawn
like Heaven coming to *us*; why snow

doesn't last forever and what
forever is anyway, wanting four sides
or an axis, something sensible
as science to his twelve-year-old mind.

His grandmother replies, says we will
be taken like Elijah in the rapture.
He equates it to alien abduction,
to the disappearance of Jack

up the beanstalk or Alice into the mirror,
remembering other worlds he has visited
in his imagination, picturing God
at the computer, His finger on delete.

He tells her his teacher says we are
seventy-two percent water, as he exhales
on the window pane, writes his name,
explains the existence of moisture

that forms, then evaporates, the snow
beginning to leave, little by little,
as breaths of steam ride a stream
of sunlight into opening clouds.

Fire Ants

Then shall two be in the field;
the one shall be taken, and the other left.
Matthew 24:40

Cleaning the driveway today,
she swept away an entire ant village,
scattered sand for yards, took
long brushes with the broom,
sent them flying into air. Some
swarmed her weapon, others
darted into the grass, confused.

She regrets killing any creature,
no matter how small, wiping out
work that must have taken
half their brief lifetimes, wonders
what they believe her to be,
a deity to them who swoops down
for no reason with what must

resemble hurricanes or dust storms.
She scratches the swelling bite mark
on her arm, suffered as she bent down
to pull out a weed, muses…if we are
like ants, not expecting to be snatched
away, going about our day, God
a larger being just clearing Her path.

Assisi in December

For what is the nature of your life? Why, it is but a mist,
which appears for a short time and then is seen no more.

James 4:14

Francesco doesn't know
what to pray for, as he stares
into winter's deep sky, craving
some miracle in solitude
while snowflakes fall.
He scrapes their small deaths
off his shoes, sits by the fire,
drifts in and out of sleep.

There's always ways to waste time,
he reminds the rabbit, lost
in the crevice of his arm.
Mornings, he worships birds
from his window, imagines
fields of yellow mustard
and red poppies, still hooked
on the drug of dreams.

Winter has no expectations of him,
unlike spring, when the world
is sweet with rain and reasons, or
summer with so many questions,
always wanting a yes or a no.
His frown, warmed by the sun,
fades with frost's glossy wings,
sighs fog the cold glass, each
breath exhaling its gossamer blossom.

Outside, Looking In

The world looks at her through the windows
of her kitchen, her bedroom, the den,
the spotless glass panels on the front door.

Trees peer through sparkling panes, dew
dawdles on the morning sill, watches her
going about daily chores. Each room knows

her routine, dusting books she hasn't read,
wiping letters on the simulated-leather Bible
cluttered with prayers, cleaning every corner.

There's a clock in her mind. She wakes up early
each day to watch fragile fragments
of frost, their tiny interlaced faces wanting in,

each windowpane framing the sun, fleeting things,
a broken butterfly's wing, paint peeling on a ledge,
the gaze of a dawn with everything in it.

Every now and then she raises the sash,
holds out a hand, washes it in rain.
Birthdays come and go like ordinary air.

Night waits as she finishes her work.
She always leaves the door unlocked
because she believes she has nothing

of value, no grand dreams that change you,
only clean floors that shine with time
and solitude with its certain seedy loveliness.

Journey

See, I am making all things new....
Revelations 21:5

I see the world from behind two blades,
windshield wipers that never quite clean
the crust of an insect or let go
of a piece of leaf caught in the hinge.
The clock on the dashboard is wrong.

Music from the radio keeps time
with the rain, never breaking rhythm,
raspy song of rubber, fast on the highway.
On my journey, you are a distant place,
the road empty of others. I pass the dark

buildings, vacant lots; listen to my breath,
block out the pounding sounds
on the pavement, hear my own heart beat.
I know the feeling of being inside,
inside the lamplight beginning to burn

as I turn the corner of your street, inside
the cool walls of your bedroom, inside
the heat of the 40-watt bulb by your head
inside the skin of your sheets, inside
the space between desire and sleep, where

all that is fragile has entered you, spread
across your flesh like wrinkles, wound
through your hair like gray. You whisper
"stay," to the small of my palm, my cheek,
to all I thought was without need.

LINDA ANNAS FERGUSON is the author of five collections of poetry, including *Bird Missing from One Shoulder* (WordTech Editions, 2007); *Stepping on Cracks in the Sidewalk* (Finishing Line Press, 2006); *Last Chance to Be Lost* (Kentucky Writers' Coalition, 2004); and *It's Hard to Hate a Broken Thing* (Palanquin Press, University of S.C. Aiken, 2002). She was the 2005 Poetry Fellow for the South Carolina Arts Commission and served as the 2003-04 Poet-in-Residence for the Gibbes Museum of Art in Charleston, S.C. A recipient of the Poetry Fellowship of the South Carolina Academy of Authors, she is a member of the Academy's Board of Governors. She was a featured poet for the Library of Congress Poetry at Noon Series. Her work is archived by Furman University Special Collections in the James B. Duke Library. A North Carolina native, she now resides in Charleston, SC. Visit her website at www.lindaannasferguson.com.

About the Cover Artist

BEE BRADY is a photographer from London whose emotional self-portraits and landscapes document her exploration of the places around her new countryside home. This record of a city girl in a dark rural idyll was the theme of her first solo exhibition at the 2009 Arts Festival in Faringdon, Oxfordshire, and her first book, *My Land*. Bee's photography has appeared in two books of female self-portraiture, *She Took Her Own Picture* and *In Her Own Image*. Her work was used to advertise The Belfast Film Festival, and has been used in several other advertising campaigns across the world through Getty Images.

Visit Bee online:
http://beebradyphotography.blogspot.com/